Earth: Fast Changes

Table of Contents

by Erin Fry

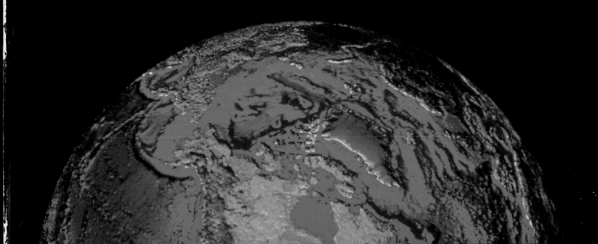

Introduction

May 18, 1980. The sun is shining brightly in a clear sky. Then, at 8:32 A.M., a **volcano** (vahl-KAY-noh) in Washington explodes. The **force** of the volcano is awesome. In minutes, one side of the mountain is torn away. Super-hot **lava** (LAH-vuh) shoots out of the volcano. Material from the volcano is found in eleven states. Entire glaciers on the face of the mountain are melted. Thousands of animals die.

This is Mount St. Helens. When it **erupted** (ih-RUP-ted) in 1980, it was the biggest volcano eruption ever in the United States.

How can Earth change so quickly? Volcanoes are very powerful forces of nature. So are **earthquakes** (ERTH-kwakes) and big storms. They can move mountains, soil, trees, water, and everything else in just seconds!

In this book, you will explore some of those fast changes. You could be amazed!

▲ The surface of Earth is constantly changing shape. This is Mount St. Helens erupting in 1980.

Earthquakes

I t was early, 5:12 A.M., on an April morning in 1906. Most people were still asleep when the city of San Francisco was hit by one of the worst earthquakes on record. In less than one minute, the ground moved more than twenty feet. Dozens of buildings were flattened. Thousands lost their lives. The city burned for days following the earthquake.

▲ San Francisco in 1906, after the earthquake

Primary Source

The writer Jack London witnessed the 1906 San Francisco earthquake. This is what he wrote: "San Francisco is gone. Nothing remains of it but memories ... great stores and newspaper buildings, the hotels and the palaces ... are all gone."

Why Does Earth Quake?

Earth has four major layers. The outer layer is the crust. It includes the ground and the ocean floor. The crust is broken up into huge pieces called **plates**. These plates move all the time. They float on the mantle (MAN-tul). The mantle's upper part is red-hot, melted rock.

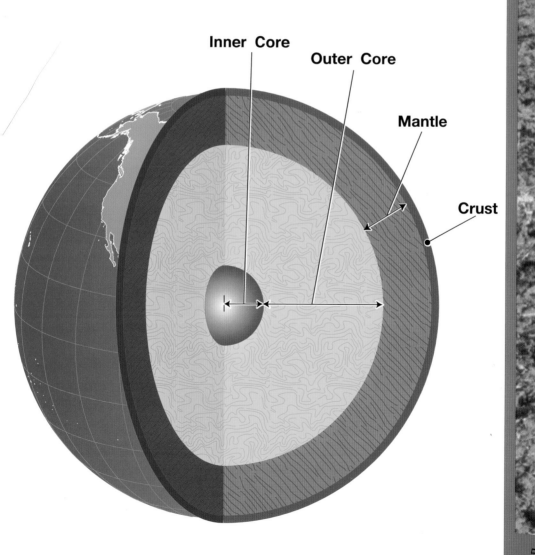

Inner Core

Outer Core

Mantle

Crust

The crust has many cracks in it. The cracks, or breaks, are called **faults** (FAULTS). When rocks get stuck along a fault, the plates keep moving. The plates push hard against the rocks. If the rocks break, the plates move suddenly, and Earth's crust starts to shake. This is an earthquake.

Earthquakes also happen when one plate sinks under another one, or when plates crash or grind past each other.

Types of Earthquakes

A. Blocks of rock move up or down along a crack.

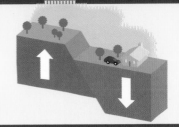

B. One block of rock slides up and over the other.

C. Rocks scrape sideways and sometimes up and down.

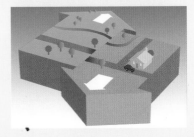

The point where the earthquake begins is the focus. Directly above is the epicenter (EH-pih-sen-ter). The plates slide along a fault. They give off energy in the form of waves. Under the ground, the waves move in all directions.

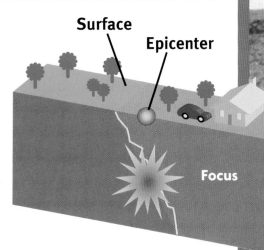

Scientists watch larger faults carefully. Earthquakes are likely to happen there again.

It's a Fact

Chinese Earthquake Predictor
The continent of Asia has the most earthquakes. Two thousand years ago, the Chinese people invented this tool to predict earthquakes. The dragons had little metal balls in their mouths. When an earthquake started, most people didn't feel it immediately. However, the little balls very noisily rolled out of the dragons' mouths and into the toads' mouths.

Where Earth Changes

Earthquakes happen every day somewhere on Earth. The force of an earthquake can start landslides and mudslides. Mud, rocks, and trees tumble down slopes. The shape of the land changes. But most earthquakes are small and cause no damage.

▲ The most active quake zone in the world is around the Pacific Ocean. California, Hawaii, and Alaska are in this zone.

They Made a Difference

Scientists use a seismograph (SIZE-muh-graf). This machine measures and records the strength of earthquakes from as far as 600 miles (966 kilometers) away! In 1935, Charles Richter (RIK-ter) invented a **scale**. The scale helped scientists read the seismograph more easily. Richter's scale goes from 1 to 9. It measures the **magnitude** (MAG-nih-tood), or power, of a quake. Each number is ten times stronger than the number below it. For example, a magnitude 4 earthquake shakes ten times more than a magnitude 3 quake. Earthquakes of 7 or above on this scale usually mean a lot of damage.

8

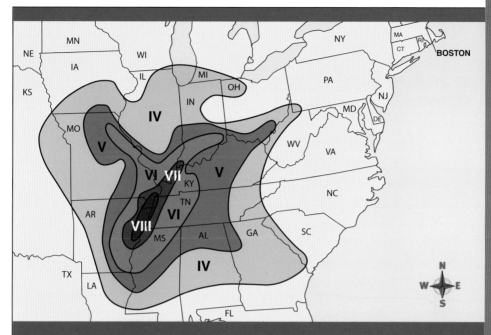

▲ The quake in New Madrid, Missouri, was felt at least 1,000 miles away in Boston, Massachusetts. Bells rang in church towers there!

Closer to Home

In 1811 and 1812, three very big earthquakes struck near New Madrid, Missouri. They changed Earth's surface more than any other earthquake in North America. They might have shown 8.0 or higher on today's Richter scale. Large areas of land sank and new lakes formed. Thousands of acres of forests were destroyed. One quake even changed the course of the Mississippi River!

9

Measuring the Effects of an Earthquake

When an earthquake happens, it is often felt far away. Does one place along the fault have more damage? Find out for yourself.

▶ **What You Need**

1. an empty box—like a shoe box.
2. about three tablespoons of lentils or small, dried beans
3. a ruler
4. a clock with a second hand, or a timer
5. paper, pencil, and a marker
6. a partner
7. floor with a rug

▶ **What You Do**

1. Make a chart to record what you see:

Place	Effects of Tapping the Box
Place 1 nearest the epicenter	
Place 2	
Place 3 farthest from the epicenter	

2. Place the box on a rug on the floor. Put a small handful of dried beans at each end of the box. Put a small handful of beans in the middle of the box.
3. Number the places 1, 2, and 3.
4. Hold the far end of the box firmly. Lightly tap on the other end. Keep tapping for 30 seconds.

5. Ask your partner to record on the chart what he or she sees in the box.
6. Switch places and do steps 2–5 again.
7. Compare what you saw.

If you are still curious about earthquakes, you might try to figure this out: If an earthquake lasts a short time, will its effects be different than one that lasts a long time?

▲ Huge waves spread along the Indian Ocean and South China Sea. Waves spread to the coast of Africa. The waves covered small islands and moved tons of sand and earth. The land changed very quickly.

The Tsunami of 2004

The early morning of December 26, 2004, started out peacefully in South Asia. Then a huge 9.3 magnitude earthquake struck deep in the Indian Ocean. The quake caused a **tsunami** (soo-NAH-mee), or giant wave. The tsunami spread across the Indian Ocean for 2,796 miles (4,500 kilometers).

Its speed was 500 miles (805 kilometers) per hour! As it reached the shore, it slowed. But the waves grew taller. The first wave was 30 feet (9.1 meters) tall when it crashed on shore.

1. Solve This

A tsunami is traveling at a speed of 300 miles (482.7 kilometers) per hour. From a distance of 100 miles (160.9 kilometers) offshore, about how long will it take for the tsunami to hit land?

People along the Indian Ocean had no warning. Right before the big wave hit, a strange thing happened. The ocean suddenly pulled back. People could see the ocean floor. They saw fish flopping on the exposed ground. Then a wall of water slammed onto the coast. Property was destroyed. More than 200,000 people died. Now scientists are working hard to make better warning systems.

▲ The tsunami in South Asia changed people's lives. In a matter of moments, it also changed the appearance of the land.

Volcanoes

One of the world's most active and most famous volcanoes is Mount Vesuvius. When it erupted in A.D. 79, it completely covered the ancient city of Pompeii.

Like most volcanoes, Vesuvius looks like a mountain. A cone forms at the top when materials blast out of the opening. Ash, solid rock, and **magma** (MAG-muh), or liquid rock, erupt through the cone.

Below Earth's crust, red-hot rock, called magma, rises up. Force from below pushes it up toward the surface. A volcano forms when magma and hot gases escape through openings in the surface of Earth.

It's a Fact

Ring of Fire

More than half of the world's volcanoes are located in what is known as the Ring of Fire. Most active volcanoes are in that zone.

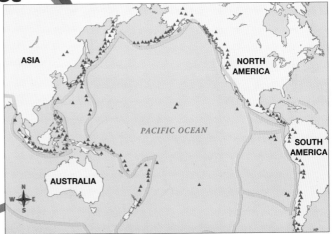

ASIA

NORTH AMERICA

PACIFIC OCEAN

SOUTH AMERICA

AUSTRALIA

N W E S

More About Mount Vesuvius

When the volcano erupted, a giant ash cloud rose 20 miles (32 kilometers) into the sky. Huge amounts of red-hot lava and rock roared down its sides. The lava destroyed everything in its path. While the A.D. 79 eruption of Mount Vesuvius is the most famous, the volcano has erupted many times since. Though it has been quiet since 1944, Mount Vesuvius will probably erupt again in the future.

The First Volcanoes

Long ago, people thought volcanoes erupted because gods were angry with humans. The word *volcano* comes from Vulcan, the Roman god of fire.

▲ 1780 painting of Vesuvius erupting

Careers in Science

Do you like to spend time outdoors? Are you curious about how Earth works? You might become a volcanologist (vahl-kuh-NAH-luh-jist). These scientists explore volcanoes all over the world. They study how and why volcanoes erupt. They also look for signs that might tell when a volcano is getting active. They study everything that comes out of a volcano and how Earth is affected.

New Islands

Sometimes, a volcano can start new islands. Many volcanoes are located on the floor of the ocean. Most of the magma does not reach open air. But volcanic rock and ash, as well as billowing clouds of steam, do. If the pile of rock and ash is capped by lava, erosion will be prevented and new land will form.

It's a Fact

Newest Island

In 1963, a volcano formed a new island off the coast of Iceland. The new island was named Surtsey (SERT-say). Seeds that traveled on the water or in the air took root on the island. Now, it is a nature preserve. People come to study what kinds of animals and plants grow there.

▲ the island of Surtsey being formed

▲ the island of Surtsey as it looks now

Affecting the Weather and Earth

Some volcano blasts are powerful enough to change the weather in the area. For months after such an eruption, there can be heavy winds and rain.

Volcano gases and dust can travel all around the world. This changes Earth's weather. The dust can block sunlight, so Earth cools down. Over hundreds of years, the dust could cause global cooling or another ice age.

▼ These computer-enhanced images show the Philippines before and after the 1991 eruption of Mount Pinatubo.

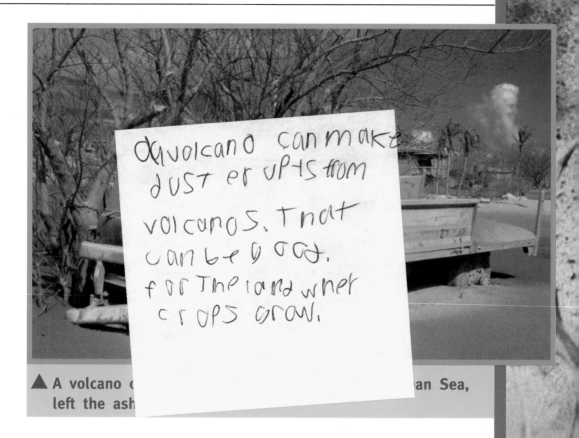

A volcano [handwritten note obscures text] an Sea, left the ash [text obscured]

Handwritten note:
a volcano can make dust er upts from volcanos. That can be good. for The land wher crops grow.

Some Good News

Sometimes, only a small amount of ash and dust erupts from a volcano. That can be good for the land where crops grow. For example, Karisimbi (kar-ih-SIM-bee) is an active volcano in East Africa. The land around it is very rich, thanks to help from the volcano. Good crops grow there, and everyone can eat.

✓ Point Make Connections

Read more about the 2004 tsunami at your school library or local library. Find out how people around the world have helped tsunami victims.

Storms

You click on the TV just in time for the weather report. A tropical (TRAH-pih-kul) storm is headed to the Florida coast. If the wind speed goes up much more, the storm will become a **hurricane** (HER-ih-kane).

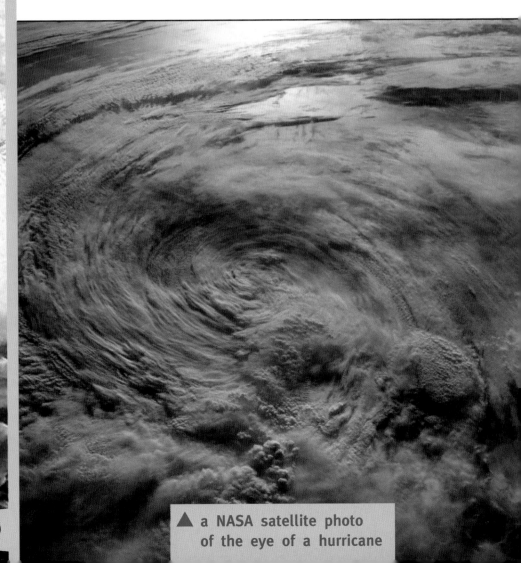

▲ a NASA satellite photo of the eye of a hurricane

Hurricanes

Hurricanes start over a warm ocean. At first, they are small thunderstorms. Heat from the water speeds up the wind. Winds and small drops of water in the air move around and around very fast. So the storm gets stronger.

If the winds blow faster than 73 miles (117 kilometers) per hour, then the storm becomes a hurricane. A hurricane can grow to be more than 100 miles (161 kilometers) wide.

2. Solve This

A hurricane is 80 miles from land. The weather forecaster says it will hit land in 30 minutes. How fast is the hurricane traveling?
Answer in miles per hour.

21

▲ This photo of Hurricane Ivan was taken from the International Space Station.

A Hurricane Hits Land

Hurricanes can change the shape of Earth's surface very quickly. They can hit land with winds that tear huge trees from the ground. Heavy rains wash away the soil that plants need to grow. High waves break along the shore and take away dirt, rocks, and sand.

▲ Twenty-foot-high hurricane waves crash against the shore in Florida.

ATLANTIC OCEAN

This map shows the path of Hurricane Ivan. Hurricanes hit the Caribbean (kair-ih-BEE-un) islands every year. From June to November, this part of the world stays ready. ▲

Storm Surges

Hurricane Ivan struck the coast of Alabama in 2004. Winds measured at 120 miles (192 kilometers) per hour pounded the shoreline. Heavy rains caused big floods.

But some of the worst damage came from Hurricane Ivan's **storm surge** (STORM SERJ). A storm surge is a rise in the level of the sea caused by the winds of a hurricane.

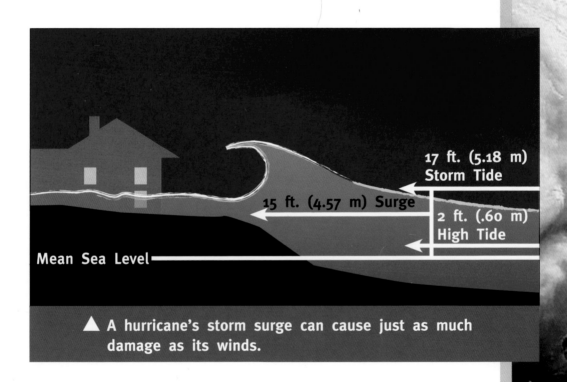

17 ft. (5.18 m) Storm Tide

15 ft. (4.57 m) Surge

2 ft. (.60 m) High Tide

Mean Sea Level

▲ A hurricane's storm surge can cause just as much damage as its winds.

A storm surge can rise up to 26 feet (8 meters) high. Hurricane Ivan's storm surge was about 16 feet (4.9 meters) high. The tall waves carried lots of sand and rocks into the ocean. They changed the shape of the coastline along two states!

It's a Fact

More than one hurricane can happen at the same time. And they move around a lot. Storm trackers needed a way to tell everyone which hurricane they were talking about. The problem was solved by naming them. Names of the worst hurricanes are never used again.

▲ This trailer park in Florida was completely wiped out in 2001 by Hurricane Andrew.

Islands Get Smaller

Islands can be very much in danger during hurricanes. Islands off the coast of North Carolina are actually losing shoreline every year.

A lighthouse built on Cape Hatteras in 1870 was 1,500 feet (460 meters) from the ocean. In 1987, it stood only 160 feet (49 meters) from the sea. In 1999, it was moved a half-mile inland to protect it.

▲ This lighthouse had to be moved inland nearly 2,600 feet (792 meters) because the earth was beginning to wash away under it.

◀ Cape Hatteras, as seen from the space shuttle *Endeavour*

▲ the capital of Honduras after Hurricane Mitch

One Huge Change

Hurricanes can also produce enough rain to cause mudslides. In 1998, Hurricane Mitch hit parts of Central America. In Nicaragua (nih-kuh-RAH-gwuh), heavy rains poured for days. A giant section, or part, of the Casita volcano crashed down in a mudslide. Mudflows covered entire villages.

Everyday Science

The Power of Heavy Rain

Hurricanes aren't the only storms that can change Earth's surface. Sometimes, heavy rain is enough. Heavy rains are a common cause of mudslides. A whole hillside can begin to slide if it becomes very wet.

Hurricanes Around the World

Hurricanes have other names in different parts of the world. Sometimes they are called cyclones (SY-klonez). In the ⋯⋯ of the Pacific Oc⋯ ⋯led typhoons (ty⋯ ⋯LE-yunz) call the ⋯

handwritten note: Some call Then different noms.

T⋯ spin⋯ of th⋯ they⋯ the e⋯ the o⋯

▲ satellite image of Hurricane Andrew

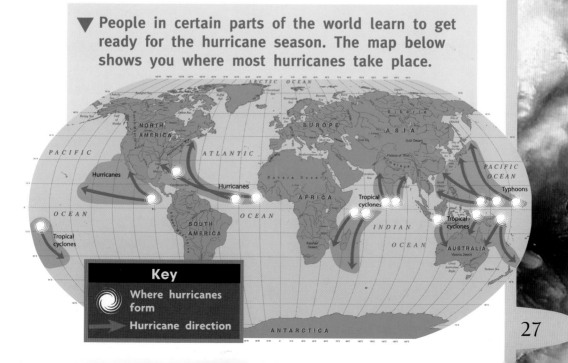

▼ People in certain parts of the world learn to get ready for the hurricane season. The map below shows you where most hurricanes take place.

Key
Where hurricanes form
Hurricane direction

Monsoons

Every year starting in June, **monsoons** (mahn-SOONZ) bring four months of heavy rain to India. Monsoons are very powerful winds that change direction. They can cause flooding and landslides. Entire hillsides can be washed away after days of heavy rains. Flooding near river banks can destroy crops.

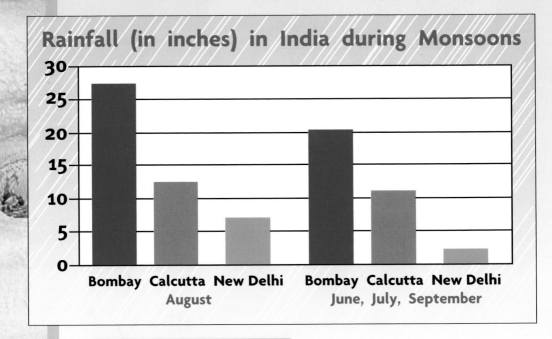

Rainfall (in inches) in India during Monsoons

3. Solve This

Which city in India gets the most rain during the monsoon season? How many inches total does this city get in these four months?

✔ Point Picture It

A wave taller than a house crashes onto the shore. Draw what this might look like. Be sure to show how a wave like this could change Earth's surface.

Conclusion

It may seem like Earth does not change very much. But earthquakes, volcanoes, and huge storms cause important changes. And they can do it quickly. They can cause landslides, mudslides, and floods. Sometimes, they can create waves and winds that move rocks, dirt, and sand from one place to another.

Will those forces keep changing Earth? Yes, they will. We cannot stop Earth's changes. But we can learn about them. We can find ways to reduce the amount of damage caused by these natural forces.

Talk It Over

Use the chart to help you summarize the three types of natural disasters. Name changes that all three of them can cause.

Disaster Effects

Earthquakes	Volcanoes	Hurricanes
faults, mudslides, rockslides, tsunamis; formation of lakes; forests destroyed	formation of islands, and others disappear; new craters; lava flows; forests destroyed	floods, forests destroyed; mudslides; land wears away

◀ The Oued Fodda (WED FOH-duh) Fault in Algeria (al-JEER-ee-uh) shows what the land looks like when one block of rock hangs over another one.

Glossary

earthquake   (ERTH-kwake) shaking of Earth's crust (page 3)

erupt   (ih-RUPT) burst out with great force (page 2)

fault   (FAULT) a crack in the surface of Earth where rocks slide past each other during an earthquake (page 6)

force   (FORS) a pushing or pulling action that can change the shape of something (page 2)

hurricane   (HER-ih-kane) a large, powerful storm with high winds that forms over an ocean (page 20)

lava   (LAH-vuh) red-hot, liquid rock that has reached Earth's surface from a volcano (page 2)

magma   (MAG-muh) red-hot, liquid rock under Earth's crust (page 14)

magnitude   (MAG-nih-tood) the size or power of something—in this case, the power of an earthquake (page 8)

monsoon   (mahn-SOON) a strong, violent wind that brings heavy rains to parts of Asia (page 28)

plate   (PLATE) a section of Earth's crust and upper mantle (page 5)

scale   (SKALE) a system of numbers used to measure something, such as a ruler (page 8)

storm surge   (STORM SERJ) a sudden rise in sea level caused by a storm (page 23)

tsunami   (soo-NAH-mee) a large wave caused when an earthquake happens on the ocean floor (page 12)

volcano   (vahl-KAY-noh) an opening in Earth's surface; a mountain that is formed from material that comes through this opening (page 2)

Solve This Answers

1. Page 12 20 minutes
If it takes one hour—60 minutes—to travel 300 miles, it would take 40 minutes to travel 200 miles. So it would take 20 minutes to travel 100 miles.

2. Page 21 It is traveling at 160 miles per hour. This problem has two parts.

A. You know that an hour has 60 minutes. You know that 30 minutes were spent traveling. The storm has thirty minutes (half of its hour) left to travel. 60 − 30 = 30 minutes.

B. The hurricane is at the halfway point: 80 miles from shore. You know that two halves make a whole. So: Multiply 80 x 2 = 160.

3. Page 28 Bombay. 48 inches
Compare the numbers on the graph. Bombay had the most rainfall. Add up the total rainfalls for Bombay.